INDY CARS

Sarah Tieck

Big Buddy BOOKS

Amazing Vehicles

ABDO
Publishing Company

Amazing Vehicles

VISIT US AT
www.abdopublishing.com

Published by ABDO Publishing Company, 8000 West 78th Street, Edina, Minnesota 55439.

Printed in the United States.

Coordinating Series Editor: Rochelle Baltzer
Contributing Editors: Megan M. Gunderson, BreAnn Rumsch, Marcia Zappa
Graphic Design: Deb Coldiron, Marcia Zappa
Cover Photograph: *Shutterstock*: Anson Hung
Interior Photographs/Illustrations: *AP Photo*: AP Photo (pp. 29, 30), Paul Beaty (pp. 13, 29), Michael Conroy (p. 25), Michael Conroy, File (p. 25), Darron Cummings (p. 27), David Duprey (p. 9), Bill Fundaro (p. 11), Russ Hamilton (p. 17), Ben Margot (p. 5), Seth Rossman (p. 27), John Ulan/THE CANADIAN PRESS (p. 7); *Getty Images*: Robert Laberge (p. 19), Donald Miralle (pp. 15, 21); *Shutterstock*: Lori Carpenter (p. 9), Anson Hung (pp. 4, 7, 8, 12, 21), Todd Taulman (p. 23).

Library of Congress Cataloging-in-Publication Data

Tieck, Sarah, 1976-
  Indy cars / Sarah Tieck.
    p. cm. -- (Amazing vehicles)
  ISBN 978-1-60453-542-6
  1. Indy cars--Juvenile literature. I. Title.

TL236.T55 2009
629.228--dc22

                              2009001759

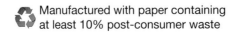
Manufactured with paper containing
at least 10% post-consumer waste

CONTENTS

FAST FACT: Indy cars are used in the Indianapolis 500. They got their name from this famous race.

GET MOVING

Imagine racing around a track in an Indy car. Warm air blows past you as you speed around curves. The crowd cheers as you go faster!

Have you ever seen an Indy car up close? Many parts work together to make it move. An Indy car is an amazing vehicle!

Indy cars compete in races. They go very fast over many miles.

WHAT IS AN INDY CAR?

An Indy car is a type of open-wheel race car. Most cars have wheels below the body or tucked into the frame. But, an open-wheel race car has wheels off the sides of its body.

Another type of open-wheel race car is the Formula One. These cars are used for racing in Europe.

Indy cars race as part of the Indy Racing League.

Indy cars are known for their smooth, soft rubber tires. Indy car tires are 10 to 15 inches (25 to 38 cm) wide. They are made to **grip** the road at fast speeds.

Indy car tires last less than 100 miles (161 km). So, a car uses several sets of tires during a 500-mile (805-km) race.

Indy car tires spin so fast that they create heat. During a race, they can reach the temperature of boiling water! This makes them wear out faster than standard tires.

A CLOSER LOOK

The main body of an Indy car is called a chassis. It is made up of a frame, central parts, and an outer shell. The chassis helps **protect** the driver.

Indy cars are made from strong but lightweight parts. This helps them travel at high speeds during long races. Open-wheel races are some of the fastest in the world.

INDY CARS

Wings help an Indy car balance as it moves. Different styles of wings are meant for different racetracks.

The **air intake** helps cool the engine.

The **steering wheel** is hard to turn. Because there is no power steering, drivers use their strength to turn the wheel.

Companies often pay for space on a car's **chassis**. Putting their name or logo on a race car helps them get business.

Indy car **tires** are smooth. Unlike the tires on most other vehicles, Indy car tires do not have a raised pattern.

FAST FACT: Indy cars can move with the same force as a space shuttle taking off! And, they can travel the length of a football field in about one second.

HOW DOES IT MOVE?

An Indy car moves when its large wheels spin. But, the wheels need power to turn.

The Indy car's engine supplies that power. It provides enough force to turn an **axle**. This axle is connected to the car's rear wheels. When it spins, the wheels turn.

An Indy car can move in different directions. To control its direction, the driver turns the **steering** wheel.

Sometimes, Indy cars reach 220 miles (354 km) per hour! Even on the freeway, most cars only go about 65 miles (105 km) per hour.

Indy car engines burn a fuel called ethanol. Ethanol provides more power than gasoline without overheating the engine.

POWERFUL ENGINES

Indy cars are made to go very fast. Because of this, they have powerful engines.

Indy car engines are built into the car's frame. To go faster, the driver pushes a pedal. The **steering** wheel has buttons, dials, and displays. These also help the driver control the car.

BEHIND THE WHEEL

Only **professionals** can drive Indy cars. It takes skill to drive safely at such fast speeds. Drivers practice and **compete** for many years. Over time, they earn more opportunities to race.

Indy cars are exciting to watch! But, driving an Indy car can be unsafe. If drivers lose control, they can be badly hurt. For **protection**, drivers wear special suits that cover their bodies. They also wear helmets with **visors**.

Indy racing helmets have special features. Some have a hose for the driver to drink through while racing. To get a drink, the driver pushes a button on the steering wheel.

17

RACETRACKS

Indy cars race on tracks. There are Indy racetracks in the United States, Canada, and Japan!

Most Indy racetracks are oval shaped. But tracks can also be street circuits, road courses, and rounded triangle shapes.

Racers must earn their starting spot for each race. Pole position is the best position at the start of the race. Usually, this is the inside car in the front row.

PIT STOPS

Indy car races can be very long. The speed and hot racetrack wear down the cars. So, an Indy car usually needs fuel, new tires, and other work.

During a race, drivers pull into areas called pits for breaks. A wall separates the pit lane from the racetrack. Inside the pit lane, there are garages, tools, and car parts. There are also **hoses** with air and fuel.

FAST FACT: Because of pit stops, cars carry less fuel during the race. This makes them lighter and faster.

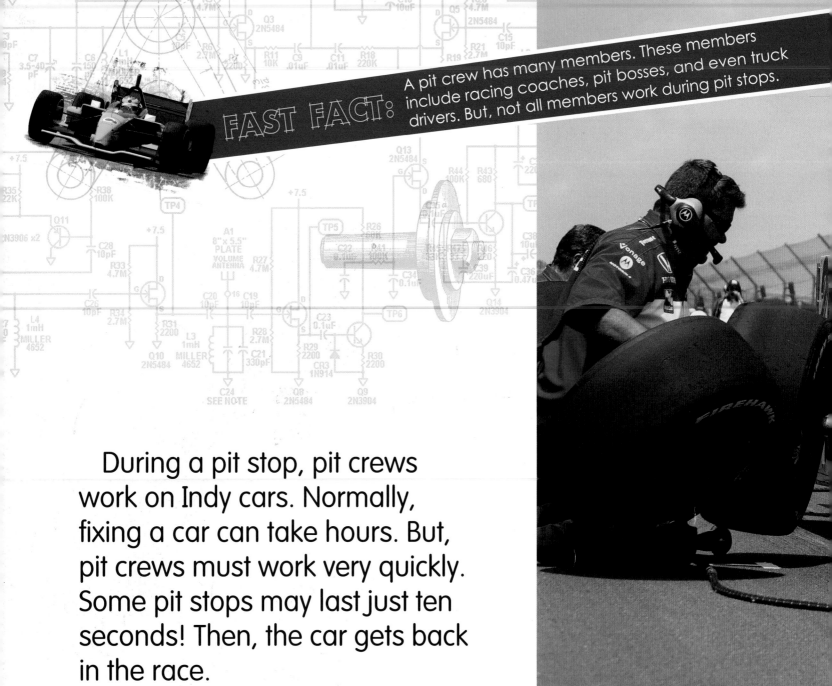

During a pit stop, pit crews work on Indy cars. Normally, fixing a car can take hours. But, pit crews must work very quickly. Some pit stops may last just ten seconds! Then, the car gets back in the race.

Only six pit crew members are allowed
in the pit lane to work on a car.

FAST DRIVERS

There have been many famous Indy car drivers over the years. Indy car drivers race with teams. Team owners control prize and **sponsor** money. And, they pay for cars, crews, and other expenses.

Mario Andretti was a successful racer from the 1960s to the 1990s. Over the years he won many races and **championships**. He is famous for his accomplishments.

Scott Dixon is considered one of the most successful Indy car drivers of 2008. He won many races that year, including the Indianapolis 500.

Mario Andretti no longer races, but his family members do. In 2006, his grandson Marco Andretti finished second in the Indianapolis 500.

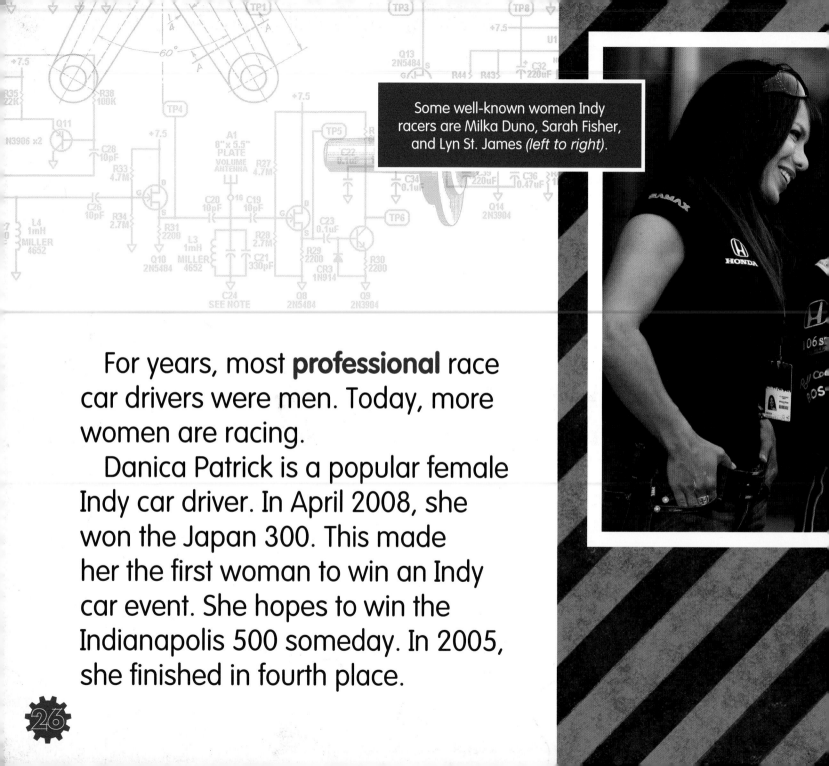

Some well-known women Indy racers are Milka Duno, Sarah Fisher, and Lyn St. James *(left to right)*.

For years, most **professional** race car drivers were men. Today, more women are racing.

Danica Patrick is a popular female Indy car driver. In April 2008, she won the Japan 300. This made her the first woman to win an Indy car event. She hopes to win the Indianapolis 500 someday. In 2005, she finished in fourth place.

Danica Patrick won a 2008 Nickelodeon Kids' Choice Award. She was named favorite female athlete.

PAST TO PRESENT

The first Indy cars went about 75 miles (120 km) per hour. Today, some travel more than 200 miles (320 km) per hour!

These open-wheel race cars are mostly used in Indy Racing League events. They are made strong to **compete** in long races. Indy cars are amazing vehicles!

Over the years, Indy cars have become faster, lighter, and more powerful. Today's cars use computers and other technology.

BLAST FROM THE PAST

The first Indianapolis 500 race took place on May 30, 1911. Today, the yearly Indy 500 is still considered the most popular Indy Racing League event.

This open-wheel race takes place at the Indianapolis Motor Speedway in Speedway, Indiana. There, drivers race for 500 miles (805 km) in one day. They drive 200 laps around the track!

IMPORTANT WORDS

axle (AK-suhl) a bar on which a wheel or a pair of wheels turns.

championship a contest held to find a first-place winner.

compete to take part in a contest between two or more persons or groups.

grip to hold tightly.

hose a bendable tube through which liquids or gasses can pass.

professional (pruh-FEHSH-nuhl) working for money rather than for pleasure.

protect (pruh-TEHKT) to guard against harm or danger.

sponsor a person or a group that agrees to pay expenses for the activities of another person or group.

steer to guide or control a moving vehicle.

visor a part of a helmet that can be pulled down to cover the face.

WEB SITES

To learn more about Indy cars, visit ABDO Publishing Company online. Web sites about Indy cars are featured on our Book Links page. These links are routinely monitored and updated to provide the most current information available.

www.abdopublishing.com

31

INDEX